"This is a geography painted against
against geography itself. an orchard becomes a dzonot becomes a rose
becomes a collaborative song between dreamer and bird that bleeds
across borders. I was shown ruins through mirrors, nerve endings
that survive demolition and burnings and hide underground amongst
currents. Angel has given us a guide through the dimension just a breath
away from the veil."

—TATIANA LUBOVISKI-ACOSTA

"*RoseSunWater* is a vast and powerful record of dream traversals within
the heinous enduring legacy of imperialist colonial settler imposition
and erasure. Dreaming is a potent defense and antidote against the
violence and upheaval of such a hegemonic world process that has
continually sought to annihilate, alienate and displace. Dreams are
reality's generative portals and are an undulating medium inflecting
worlds and realms. Within heightened states of consciousness, Angel
Dominguez realizes the connective energies and resonances that are
capable of reworlding reality. Affinities of sacred presences and kinship
relationships are the reticulations of omniscience and guide the dreamer
to liberation, affirming collective radiance as necessary for survival.
This is a book of glittering intelligence and total love. I'm moved by the
depth perspectives culled at the thresholds of the sensitive membranes
of identity that coalesce future, past and present. This book breathes fire,
exudes floral eminence, dislodges tyranny with wind, water, sun and
roses: an entranced ceremony of existence."

—BRENDA IIJIMA

"Angel Dominguez's poetry is where you turn for that tender and
frightening feeling of calling to your past, to your ancestors, to the land
that bore you. What answers that call? Your own voice, in an 'echoic
familiarity,' sometimes unbearable and sometimes ecstatic in its repetitive
everyday. In *RoseSunWater*, much like in its spiritual predecessor *Black
Lavender Milk*, Dominguez writes in an ancient personal, a kind of
confessional voice that almost obsessively considers both its monumental
historicity and its often slow-going present. This is a moving and caring
book that pleads for some way to survive, some way to face the past,
present, and future of colonialism, racism, environmental degradation,
violence, and the police. Like all of Dominguez's books, it is a loving and
hurting dream."

—GABRIEL OJEDA-SAGUÉ

"*RoseSunWater* fills me with gratitude for Angel Dominguez and their gift---a brilliance limned in a superbly moving book. *RoseSunWater* instructs me in the purposes of memory, even of loss. Their grandmother's little house where he grew up, they inform us at the start 'is going to be destroyed before this book is ever finished.' Angel Dominguez travels far beyond that house to reconnoiter memory, through the past and loss. In 'the pyramids my ancestors built' in Yucatan, with their crowds of tourists, on the roads with their police roadblocks, at Merida, Tulum and the sacred Cenote del Chuhuan he renegotiates the lives that their family left behind. That little house in the Valley north of Los Angeles, for Angel Dominguez, is not a rehash of the nostalgic tropes of Romanticism. In the sacred cenote they find 'a gleaming Frito bag floating upon the matte, adventurine green algae that covers the portal now.' This book does not diminish the impact of gentrification nor the trashing of the body of the land through colonialism; instead, Angel Dominguez instructs us on the uses of memory, ritual and poetry in radically effective resistance against the gentrification of the spirit. If our childhood neighborhoods (our very childhoods themselves) are bulldozed by capital seeking an immediate return, our spirits are likewise gentrified by dislocation and loss, our restless and rootless migration to earn a living, continual movement, education, degrees and 'self-improvement.' *RoseSunWater* is antidote to the gentrification of the spirit you can hold in one hand, some sweet water.

—SESSHU FOSTER, author of *Atomik Aztex* and *City of the Future*

"The gift of *RoseSunWater* arrived to me today at 4:45PM by way of an orange quartz light. When Dominguez writes, 'All I ever wanted was to be alive,' everything in my body rearranged itself to receive this light. I welcome its beauty, which is like justice, but sublime."

—LARA MIMOSA MONTES, author of Thresholes

"'What does it mean to write a document of light?' It means this work is a mirror universe, a rose-covered portal across feeling. Through cenotes Yucatecos, Tongva territory, and the Santa Cruz mountains. You are holding a lineage, a fire the poet keeps building 'writing (remembering) beside the shelter I've made for myself in my veins, I keep trying to keep trying.' The poems become flowers that grow 'out of what's missing: rose, sun, water.' Be prepared to thread your own maps out of what you do not know and wish you could mend. Be prepared to find out how we must make a 'new sound out of this living.'"

—VICKIE VERTIZ, Author of *Palm Frond With Its Throat Cut*

Rose

Sun

Water

ANGEL DOMINGUEZ

the operating system
glossarium / unsilenced texts x kin(d)*
print//document

RoseSunWater

ISBN: 978-1-946031-89-1
Library of Congress Control Number: 2020945708

As of 2020 all titles are available for donation-only download via our Open Access Library: www.theoperatingsystem.org/os-open-access-community-publications-library/

The Operating System is a member of the **Radical Open Access Collective**, a community of scholar-led, not-for-profit presses, journals and other open access projects. Now consisting of 40 members, we promote a progressive vision for open publishing in the humanities and social sciences. *Learn more at:* http://radicaloa.disruptivemedia.org.uk/about/

This text was set in Minion, Albion, Freight Neo, and OCR-A Standard.

<u>Cover image description</u>: A photo taken by the author of their favorite window in their grandmother's house, 14711 Saticoy St. in Van Nuys, California, which has since been destroyed and replaced with expensive, ugly apartments. There is a soft golden light gently floating into the house through the textured window illuminating the delicate lace patterns of the sheer, rose pink curtains. This is the window the author's entire family looked out at one point or another. So much of the authors life happened in this window. This photograph is the part of the home that means most to the author. A portal to the future. The author hopes that it too can be a portal for you.

Books from The Operating System are distributed to the trade by via Ingram, with additional production by Spencer Printing, in Honesdale, PA, in the USA.

Your support makes our publications, platform and programs possible! We <3 You.

the operating system
brooklyn & worldwide
www.theoperatingsystem.org

Rose

Sun

Water

Para Mamá, la flor mas fuerte de mi familia

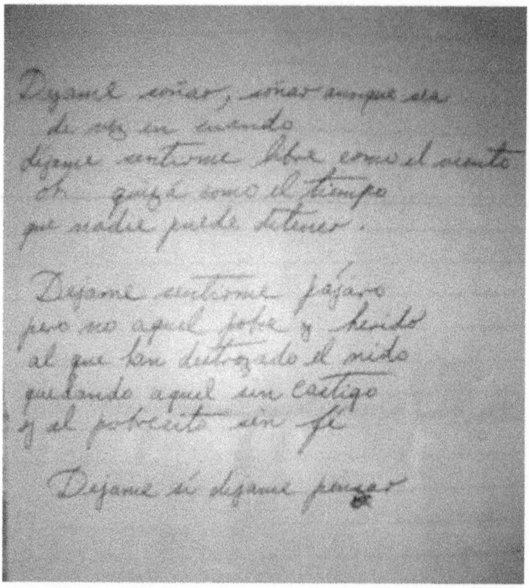

Déjame soñar, soñar aunque sea
de vez en cuando
déjame sentirme libre como el viento
oh quizá como el tiempo
que nadie puede detener.

Déjame sentirme pájaro
pero no aquel pobre y herido
al que han destrozado el nido
quedando aquel sin castigo
y al pobrecito sin fé

Déjame sí déjame pensar

Figure 1: My grandmother, Mamá sends me this poem she wrote; we try and finish together, here.

I was looking for something to soften living.
The collapse of it. The reach of it.

—NATHANAËL
(The Sorrow and the Fast of It)

that devotional organ,
my memory.
I remember.

—Rory Allen Phillip Ferreira

Home is never here for very long.

—Gabriel Ojeda-Sagué
(Losing Miami)

Déjame soñar, sonar aunque sea
de vez en cuando
déjame sentirme libre como el tiempo
que nadie puede detener.

Déjame sentirme pájaro
pero no aquel pobre y herido
al que le han destrozado el nido
quedando aquel sin castigó
y el pobrecito sin fe.

Lo que quiero, es volar
Lejos, muuuy lejos.
de cuidad en cuidad
de pueblo en pueblo
y recoger de las gentes
amor y cariño

regarlo por todo el camino
y mostrarle a el mundo enteró
que todavía existe amor y cariño,

¿Qué son los sueños? Siempre estoy buscando la lengua con la que pueda descubrir o inventar las palabras para manifestar lo que veo, lo que siento y lo que soy: un sonámbulx. Y lo que quiero decir es que la vida también es un tipo de sueño; y cuando se acaba nos despertamos otra vez, en otro siglo, con otro cuerpo y con la misma canción, el cariño del planeta y la alegría del universo. Siempre soñando, mandando besitos al futuro, hablando con los ancestros, que no se olvidan de las canciones de la sangre, de los secretos del cielo, de que nosotros somos la Ceiba —como una cadena, como la memoria de la tierra de tus abuelos, su olor— y de cómo la misma tierra puede conocerte. Sueñas como tus ancestros y vives futuros sin palabras; y la lluvia y el viento y el mar saben cómo comunicarse con tu sangre y la energía que cargas cada día. Por favor, tómate un momento para descansar, deja que las palabras de los días se evaporen de tu mente. ¿Tomaste agua hoy? Llena una taza y después cierra los ojos y llena tu mente con las flores que te entienden, con los árboles en que jugaron tus abuelos. Este momento es para ti y para ti siempre; siempre puedes regresar a la huerta de tu cuerpo. La huerta de tu memoria, la huerta de tus sueños; la huerta de los espíritus ancestros, la huerta en donde nos encontramos leyendo este libro juntos, bajo los limones, los aguacates y los pájaros, que también están soñando con otro tipo de vida, volando con sus espíritus. Aquí es donde recuperamos lo que perdimos. Lo que se olvidó para vivir. Los sueños salvan más que la vida. ¿Quieres cantar? Mi abuela me dijo que, a cantar, es conocer el mundo en la voz de tu mamá, que canta como los vientos del mar; ahora esos susurros regresan a mis alas y cuando cantas, es hora de soñar.

In a dream which is not a dream but a somnambulist reality, I swim towards the darkness that sleeps beyond what I can see. I swim beyond the safety ropes put in place, 140 meters into the reach of the Cenote, to the very lip of Xibalba, beyond light. I kick my legs into the void. Keep me still. I feel fish, or maybe spirits graze my toes and legs. I let myself fall into it. I let go. Suspended in a dream that precedes the flesh of the dreamer. I drink in this darkness, like drinking mirrors. Like drinking memory from its source. I come back to myself in the form of water. I get lost in the language, breaking the veil to breathe again.

A family of immigrants moves to the valley beyond the city. The home they find is without any record of city planning and was built in 1906 when a train still ran through this town. This house becomes a home. This home becomes a type of field, or portal. They plant fruit trees from seed; twin aguacates from the Yucatán take two decades to become a myth. The children's children become a new distance. The gardenias levitate. The pitaya blossoms a palm tree to grow upon, the lemon trees talk to one another through the night; the oranges grow less sour with every handful of salt buried beneath. New trees are planted. Many spirits leave their bodies before these words are ever written. They live with us and when you speak their names aloud they know you better. The concrete virgin grows roses out of nothing to watch over outside the kitchen. The mulberry tree plants legends in the hearts of the nearby inhabitants before bowing before the chainsaw. Later, a mango tree grows up to tell the story of these mysterious berries that had no name until Colorado dropped Mayataan words into a somnambulist ear. Years later this memory would come across as orange in its summer atmosphere, orange and creek sounds, and so small.

The Chaya emerges to nourish the keeper de la huerta antes que the house dissolves. The somnambulist calls the home an orchard because the trees allowed them to blossom and become this after-image beyond the city. The city becomes something else around the orchard. The city begins to punch holes in everyone's memory, demanding the inhabitants adapt to the ongoing invasion of everywhere else wanting to be where they are not. A sickness that spread to the somnambulist. The hunger for departure; thirsty for the transit fix. All of it imaginary. None of it real. The veins of light that become asphalt by day were a kind of comfort, now grown strange. The truth is a spiral, an ongoing descent through cycles. Each return to origin allows for a further vertical distance in memory. I sew this now to yours as you read this and we become cross-stitched and bound to one another. The city continues humming within the body despite all the silence surrounding the somnambulist.

Our blood is always buzzing.

The house is going to be destroyed before this book is ever finished.

There is nothing to do but bloom this net of neurons and temporality.

Sometimes you have to rebuild the structures within your body again and again and again and again and again and again and again and again and again.

I remember that I do not remember.

The rain comes down in thick brush strokes of spectral pigments, piles of color growing thick with movement. The trees, they dance. They twirl.

I build a house in the dead-end housing complex of my heart. The rent is cheap enough to live and every tenant is on a second chance account of some kind, my heart included.

I keep trying to build the square footage into my organs. I keep trying to form a floor plan out of memory, every time I touched my hands to those walls; feet to the floors. I am trying to remember a feeling beyond the ruin to come. There will be no pyramid. There will be no archive. Our home will become the shape of an overpriced future I can't afford. I hope every tenant's aguacates rot before they can use them.

I build a roof above a dream I've yet to have. The empty chairs manifest spirits and ancestors and we're all moving out of here before it's too late.

// DEAR ROSE, I WANT YOU TO BE SUN; BECOME WATER //

I want to save the house. Save the city. Save the sea. And still, I can't. All I can do is hold them together in my memory, piling all this language next to me, counting the containers and measuring their weight and is this sentence a year yet or does anyone ever really die? Did we ever exist at all?

Under the blue flower Scorpio moon, I dream of more time with the lemon trees; I dream of the aguacates teaching me everything they know about growing and freedom; I learn to become the house and begin to build one in the heart of my heart, and I forgot to take a brick. Wanted the memory to stick more than a maybe. I tried to make a talisman of the tragedy.

The angel's trumpets levitate and face the sky when I return to the house in dreams. It seems the structure continues to grow older in the imaginary, which may be an entangled dream, or another thing happening else-when, where the house survives. I don't assume to know the finer details of the holographic universe. I feel it sometimes and can't language fast enough to render it real. We remain parallel, never touching and yet, is that not a form of touch? Is touch not the repulsion of electrons, atoms hovering like star-systems becoming a type of distance that communicates nearness, the impossibility of connection. We become enmeshed in this language mess, and yet it's the only way I can reach you. This weary warble, the low yawn of the somnambulist waking the forest.

Surely the puncture must work both ways, if the present is ever-past, always departing...what then do we make of the future, or rather, how do we make a future out of the rubble of almost?

I mostly think I'm tethered to those sidewalks, and those cracks form an autobiography where the roses figure the concrete. I get weak knees thinking of who transfigures what and will we still live to see the rain? Look how long the days are.

I can't explain what happens to my body when I.

I keep trying to write the same book, which is not a book. There's a translation of Clarice Lispector's *Agua Viva* with a line that reads, "There is much I cannot tell you. I am not going to be autobiographical. I want to be "bio."

I too want to be bio. Here with you. What is the gesture needed to compress the body until it becomes the page? How might we (re)capture the spirits of lived experiences, here. Sometimes I hear a train call out to the ocean from the redwoods. Sometimes, a small mountain town street calls out my name with no one there. Sometimes I let myself sleep and become the rain elsewhere.

The stream is slow. These days are weeks are months and eventually the totality of time becomes compressed, or flattened by the motions of living. There's only so much scale we can comprehend before it bursts apart.

The stone is alive without my hand just as this sentence lives beyond my inevitable transmission. Or is it translation? Perhaps a transfiguration.

To become the planet again, spiraling towards the center of a larger spiral.

I got sick of writing letters to myself so I got around to talking to people.

Sometimes I feel like I might remember snippets of the future, and I can see it. In these tiny ensueños, like the mirror speckle of a minnow emerging between the murky water and its surface.

Sometimes I let myself become the rain. The rhythm grows to fit the room.

Sometimes I let the lemon trees talk to me in my dreams; mostly it's about the things they failed to mention before they're torn out of the earth, before the seed my grandmother planted reverses back into itself, back into her hands, never to be planted.

I fear the constant flattening of the city. The way these posters and flyers remain locked in a circuitous wreckage.

For a long time, I dreamt of writing a kind of entanglement - a window reflecting a window while also maintaining the image beyond each window and I'd like to think it's a bit like living.

Roses, much like rain, seem to follow me wherever I go. I've grown to love these brief salutations between living things. The rain is older than everything.

I've been thinking less and less about architectures and more about trees. The idea of trees - how the acorn is the oak, how the seed is the tree without time. Is that the book?

In my dreams, there's a language that keeps reaching outside of itself. My dreams keep telling me things about other people's dreams and sometimes I think we're entwined by this celestial rhizome that extends beyond the planet and into other planes of thinking and being and somewhere between the earth and this connection is where the writing happens, or at least, it's where the intersection occurs in such a way that opens a space for writing.

As the rain softens the particular, the trees sigh sleepy with exhale.

I warp these words to help fit the disk in my spine.

This morning I went straight to the Gulf, I meant only to sit at the beach and read, maybe write, but found myself called to the sea, so I went in. The gulf holds so many memories. Celestún, too.

This was the last beach I'd ever visit with Xix.

I'm staying two doors down from where we ate at the foot of the beach. The sea is plentiful in its fish, conch, and octopus. Celestún is perhaps most well-known for its flamingos. This morning, the swallows are buzzing like butterflies – how they soar with one another over the sea. I've traversed across the peninsula, from east to west in a sort of pilgrimage. The pelicans dive in the distance. I've driven these highways and pueblos and jungles into my body. The green shines through my blood.

Four kids go snorkeling where I was just swimming. In the sea of my lungs I taste the salt. The fishermen talk with one another. The beach is lined with shells and conches compressed from memory, less than I remember, and yet more plastic detritus. The children snorkeling are so happy. Their parents arrive and take fotos.

Somewhere in the distance beyond this beach, you sigh a little song to yourself. You soften the beach I write this on before the children emerge for air. So much of this everything opens me. Here I am, 12 years later, in the land of my Xix.

En realidad, el libro nunca está completo, porque el libro también es un tipo de sueño. Nosotros somos sonámbulxs, caminando juntos con estas palabras como un encanto. No te olvides de tomar un poco de agua. No te olvides de descansar, no importa si sólo son cinco o diez minutos. En este libro estoy construyendo otra casa, con dos hamacas y una huerta. Estoy tratando construir otro lugar en donde puedas descansar y pensar más en el misterio de la vida. Quiero que tengas tiempo de escuchar las canciones de Pedro Infante. Cierra los ojos y deja que tus pensamientos se conviertan en nubes. Recuerda los momentos más preciosos y, si tienes el tiempo, escríbelos. En esta estructura, dentro del libro, hay tiempo para escribir; hay tiempo para descansar y soñar, pero sólo si así lo quieres. Este libro es un tipo de casa.

I have
a dream

in which
my grandmother

becomes
a bird.

When the orchard begins to disappear in splotches, the dreamer and the somnambulist begin to visit the edge of the words that hold the orchard in place. They take a late summer walk through a foggy backlit labyrinth of sand and brush and tree and scents beyond what words can speak, amongst the microclimate, together as it's vanishing.

They fail to take a turn and continue on towards the sound of water. El ojo del agua emerges from off the non-path and a kind of portal is formed between here and there, between you and I, there's very little separating the energy between our nows. I'm glad we found one another in the spiral. Este agua viva.

The city is always under construction and displaces the people. There's no room for the reality beyond the image. The imaginary takes precedence and the)))))))))))))))))))) becomes erased.

How I miss the glow of the moon bathing the pitaya flowers y los limones y los pulmones de los sonámbulxs y sus sueños, su familia de soñedorxs.

Another atmospheric river runs through the mountains of Bonny Doon, flooding the orchard. The rain turns to snow and a patch of Colorado communes with its dreams of California. The roads close, the snow presses itself upon the redwoods and fruit trees. The cold presses itself against the language upon the page.

Your breath flutters like a shy ghost in the morning,

> Small imprints of familiar spirits return to your lips as
> you read this.

Unconvinced of time passing so much as our passing through it and away.

In the mirror universe that emerged along with the big bang, time flows backwards, the apartments are torn down, the earth is packed back into the lot, the trees are placed back into the soil. The house emerges, brick by brick; the Virgin de Guadalupe tiles fall back into place forming a portrait for a family to remember. We move everything back into the house; we unpack the boxes. Return the cars and fruit. There is too much to tell you. The reverse universe misses ours by a matter of 3 minutes and 33 seconds. All the matter in the holographic universe vibrates at once to reveal its openings.

Everything. Happening. Again.

It rains on the orchard for 3 seasons of water until one morning there is snow. It rains until I can't sleep. Listening to the contours of everything the rain touches; how the earth swells. I keep waiting for the power to go out. I keep waiting to learn something, or know something. To accumulate enough.

The rain hugs the orchard tighter now. The wind is coming, or already here. We arrive as always, just a second after the actual. Language works like a wink.

Spread your life across 23 hours flat and hinge the rest of your life upon it. Bet on yourself. Who will you become after the moon starts over? How will I know when the dream has ended? I remember that I do not remember. The city calls together a chorus of asphalt and lonesomeness, telephone poles punching holes in the sky with the language they carry.

Sometimes the rain asks you to stay up and write.

The rain stops at half past midnight just long enough for the full moon to come through. Sometimes you feel the moon through the ceiling and the walls. Sometimes you feel the moon through your sleep and you wake up renewed. Ready for what comes next.

// EK XIB CHAAC, THE CHAAC OF THE WEST. //

I know Chaac is always up to something. Chaac manifests south of Oregon, in the sandstone cliffs of Salt Point, big as Chichen Itza, looking out into the Pacific. Calling forth the rain. The sky forms another kind of cenote.

If you wait long enough. The fruit becomes a stone.

The stream returns to remind you that there are cycles larger than you may live to understand. The earth is a slow organ(ism) yawning in spirals behind the sun.

The canopy shyness of living organisms laced in golden light; our perception of motion: these tiny photographs, billions of moments.

This is your whole life.

Tell me about the property again.

The ground was always unusual, shaped in these larger patterns, the concrete behind the house was red and would stain your shoes or feet for a short while. The paths between this and the asphalt were made of bricks and rough pink hexagons. It was always summer in the valley. Always sweating. Always strange in the ways it would warp time; every Christmas was July with 95-degree Decembers. As a kid I would strain to see my future self, visiting me across the sidewalk, just passing through and checking in. I think I thought I might be taking care of me. Maybe I was just remembering the future.

Sometimes the spiral is a kind of Mobius strip and these cycles resonate in ways we may not understand.

Mirror seeds may take decades to germinate.

Behind the memory of the house is the house before the House. The architecture lost to insufficient memory. Some small echoes seep out into where we are now and I remember the driveway, the way my Tio would lift weights with the garage door open, or am I remembering someone else's future again?

Tell me about the trees.

I really remember the grass out front and how allergic I was. It would grow in big bunches and over time, this allergenic enemy would give way to dirt only to return again.

Before the big black gate was installed and crashed into and reinstalled there was a small aluminum-colored fence, chain-linked and bent. The sidewalk formed a triangle from the roof of a tree. This taught me the power of patience. Or perhaps it was persistence. Even the city bends if you're at it for long enough. Longer cycles. Loose lights would laugh to themselves all night as the somnambulist walked the sidewalks counting steps between the home and the house. I keep counting the steps between words wondering how language sutures or suffers or suddenly's something to something else.

The sun is going to consume us one day as we spiral towards the center of the milky way. I get tired when I think of centuries and millennia. We sleep walk through them threading energy through each other whether we want to or not and these things in life are only mirrors. Again, and again and again and again, and I keep building this fire of writing (remembering) beside the shelter I've made for myself in my veins, I keep trying to keep trying.

So why this weaving?

The rewriting written upon a translation of eradication and absence and so much loss. Recurring colonial structures maintain a constant oppression on memory, gaslighting one thousand centuries.

Mostly, I don't want to forget. There's a solidification of reality in saying something. So: writing. The living made language, which has been said a thousand times. And yet. Every flower or blossom you come across is a kind of once in a lifetime event.

This life has a way of withstanding all the language we stack on top of it.

Xix would sometimes catch parrots that were migrating from Mexico in the avocado and fruit trees. These beautiful green singing pieces of the sky. Lime green like the life surrounding the highways of the Yucatán. ¿Y qué va a pasarles a los Cenotes con todo el plástico y la basura y los turistas que no entienden que el agua es vida y más que eso? Los Cenotes son portales a Xibalba, a nuestros ancestros.

A human gliding through the sky stares out upon the horizon, noticing the curvature at the end of the world, how it wraps around itself, ouroboros, like wild peas curling along winding mountains.

The pea blossoms dream of becoming orchids and when they happen I can't tell the difference. The orchard stays with me wherever I go. Everyday another rose. Everything another pose of the familiar. Writing through the puncture wounds of memory. The gash of border boundary. The flowers that grow there, out of what's missing: rose, sun, water.

I think of the wild mountain roses that emerge every year around the anniversary of Xix's transference. A wall of roses exists on the orchard, presiding over the palm tree portal. The roses have grown together to form a wall of fragrance; they've managed to become a kind of tree, wrapped around the cherries and oaks, they've managed to kiss the sky, finding the sun first every season. When it's time to sleep again for another set of cosmic spirals la huerta rains rose petals in soft liturgy, a slow walk back to the sky.

When I visited the Yucatán in 2006, I began seeing a small black moth. It was tiny, and I first noticed it while bathing in my Tia's home, where my grandfather and I were staying during our visit. I remember the washed-out pink walls, the water; the moth. I remember how I started seeing this little fluttering spirit everywhere I went afterwards.

So much of me believes this is my Tio Pepe.

My Tio Pepe took me to eat my last torta of cochinita pibil at his favorite cart vendor before anyone else was awake. I love my Tio Pepe. He made me promise I'd come visit (I wrote "home" down immediately, I thought you should know that) Mérida before he died, and I promised him that I would.

Another reflection of an infinite nothing.

You know, I worked with people that told me about infinite galaxies in which there are "copies" of ourselves, as ourselves, exactly 3 centimeters to our left; this infinite multiplexing of the self is happening concurrent, if not coexistent with our present reality; it dimension flutters, blurs, and waves.

The event does not exist. Cat in a box. Tree in the woods. Whatever.

It's just the kind of day where you wake up to your family visiting for the first time in a decade.

It's just the kind of day where nothing gets done and

That sentence never gets finished. I go back and visit and return before the thought ever materializes. Another sentence. Another line of thought. Another jungle highway soaked in jaguar piss. Another open-palmed pig of the state offering a safe passage via bribery. Another hurricane follows me across the outline of my family; another sheet of rain asking if I'll hydroplane and stay in the land of my ancestry forever; another moment thinking, bury me where I lay. Bury a poem where I'm going.

Once again on the tarmac—once again after blue—what comes after blue, but clouds? Hard to pronounce all that sound and fury when you're nothing. All I ever wanted was to be alive. That much has always been clear to me. Even when I took the time to try and end myself over and over, eventually you learn that leaning towards oblivion is a quest for the light of life that shines thinnest.

It's hard to put what I mean into words.

It's like:

rose ocean sun ocean river spring water orchard

huerta mountain flower shoulder cloud ocean lung

orchard ocean sky thorn fire wave, sky sky sky.

It's something like flowers.

And you swallow heaven.

My dear friend tells me about an indigenous king who was told about heaven by the Spanish invasion; they asked, "*well don't you want to go to heaven? Land of milk and honey and eternal bliss?*"

The king responded:

"Do the Spanish go to heaven?"

"*But of course!*" they said, and so the King responded:

"If that's the case, I'd rather go to hell with people less cruel than you."

How do you navigate the cruelty of colonization?

How do you navigate the cruelty of a country?

How do you circumvent the cruelty of heaven?

I'm trying to remember.

Even at 30,000 ft.

I can't escape (writing.) these questions.

Sitting in front of myself,
Still lonesome still hungry
Still surviving history
Still navigating the body
its many sorrows (I wrote, sorrys).

As we
near our
destination

Cenotes of light
appear below

blooming beacons
of   Home.

I saw Magui yesterday and it was like no time passed:

"Los años se van y los años se quedan."

There are so many feelings it's hard to know where to begin.

Here, on a beach in Tulum, overlooking las ruinas, la arena como azúcar, como polvo, como mis sueños. ¿Qué es soñar vivo, con los ojos abiertos? ¿Y qué pasa cuando se enchufa estas lenguas? Qué maravilla que aquí estoy, vivo, en las tierras de mi sangre, en la playa de mis ancestros. Qué raro. ¡Maré, qué bonito! ¡Qué bueno!

Immersed in the water of my ancestry,

I stand in the sea
Until I cry
I cry until I
Laugh
I laugh until I
Am the sun.

Immersed in the water of my ancestry.

I start having memories of the last time Xix put his hand on my shoulder, pointing to an iguana,

"Eso se llama
'tu-loc'."

(Our) family, we're all storytellers.

Con mi cuerpo
en el agua
de mi sangre,

¿Quién debo ser?
¿Qué vida debo vivir?

Y de repente me fijo.
¿Porque lo estoy
preguntando en español?

¿Cuál es la lengua del mar?
¿Cuál es la lengua del sol?
Con mi cuerpo en el agua
de mis ancestros,
pregunto al agua:

¿quién debo ser?

Y de repente, empiezo a llorar. Y es como una memoria de
bastantes sueños: todo mi cuerpo en el agua —el agua de mi
vida—y siento el dolor de la Maya; y yo, ¿quién soy? Soy un
poeta y soy mestizx y también soy americanx, pero yucateco de
Los Ángeles. Y además soy humano. ¿Cuál es la vida que debo
vivir?

¿Y yo?, ¿quién soy?

Immersed in a sea of dreaming, my ancestors hold me. I stare across a far blue line. Water triggers memory, its touch, I remember the hands of my Xix walking with me, calm and patient, full of love.

Full of time, I can feel
His hands, I remember
The ruins, I remember

                                    Everything pours out of me.

My body dissolves into the sea.

                                    Everything pouring out of me.

There is so much I don't know. La arena como azúcar Glitches in pink moments; blue becomes blue becomes blue becomes bloom.

                                    The water washes me away.

The gulf in my bones
Expands.

What does it mean to write a document of light?

Everywhere I go here, there's an echoic familiarity. Everyone looks like family, and I find comfort in it.

I never feel quite at home when I'm anywhere and yet. Here I am in the land of my grandfather, in the land of my ancestors, and I finally feel at ease. There's this strange comfort that comes over me, I can't quite find the form of it. I build a nest in which I sleep.

I have a dream in which you grow your favorite flowers
                              On the windowsill of your heart.

                                        You drink more water.

                                        You get more sleep.

                              You learn to be more patient with yourself.

                    You learn to take it easy, even if only for a moment.

                    I have a dream where we are both unafraid of dying.

The sea has me in hysterics

Crying uncontrollably

Laughing riotously

Until a language of clouds emerges

                              Everything I breathe is a memory.

The energy begins to drift

With   the   next   wave.

How do I take this back with me?
How do I (re)build the house in my heart?

What will become of my liver?
What will become of my kidneys?
What will become of my teeth?
What will become of my memory?
What will become of my dreams?

What to do with all these visions?

Let it all go.
The sorrow the sadness. All of it.

En los cuerpos de mi familia vive un mar en donde las energías de la familia están transfiguradas. Se llenan con el agua del cenote en el cielo, cuando ya no tengo la fuerza suficiente para continuar a causa de todas las porquerías del país que nos quiere matar. El Cenote eterno de nuestros sueños y ancestros.

How will I learn to love myself?

Which thread? Which rope? Which weaving? Which water? Which light? All I've ever been is paper and water and

How will I learn to live without borders without flags without nationality?

I sat swinging, watching as a cyclone quietly forming over the distance of water.

Sade plays in the background as the sky draws a wavy line of wind and water connects the sea to another sea that shimmers above the planet in clouds.

The land of Chaac.

The most complicated emotion I've ever known has been joy. Tonight, I experienced something I can only describe as the sublime. It was a wash of emotions. Bliss.

The habanero opened me up to myself and brought back many memories, all at once.

In the tapestry of your blood which is a planet,

I want these notes to grow into poems.

Getting here, driving through monté y bosque and

It just kept raining. A torrential downpour.

There weren't lanes in the road so much as silent agreements and suggestions between drivers. It felt like swimming through a new body of water.

The only thing that gave me any real fear were la policía federal.

I don't trust cops in any language or land.

There was a checkpoint moment as we entered the Yucatán, leaving Quintana Roo

I couldn't quite catch everything he was saying, but there was a sentence that stayed

"*¿Todo es tranquilo?*"

His eyes were lighter than mine and lifeless.

His hands never left his rifle.

The imprint of that gun never left me either.

"*¿Quién eres?*"

¿Sabes qué? No sé. Es por eso que llegué. Y ésa es la razón por la que estoy manejando, para buscar a mi familia en donde sea que vivan; porque no entiendo quién yo soy ni quién debo ser.

¿Quién va a apagar la noche?

¿Cómo crece la curiosidad? Y, ¿qué son las palabras?

¿La lengua del corazón y la lengua de los espíritus?

¿Qué son las palabras de la sangre?

¿Cómo te voy a reconocer cuando llegue?

Wake up with the península raining pura lluvia, es como un bautismo, pero ése es un concepto de los españoles y yo soy mestizx. Y

¿qué pasó antes?

¿Cuáles fueron las bendiciones?

¿Cuáles son las palabras que mi sangre está buscando?

Since arriving I've been seeing so many spirits.

The ghosts of Maya past, one walking into the forest outside of Tulum. One sitting on the highway to Celestún, crouched in a nest of rain.

There's a deep and ancient energy here; ancestral openings connected to this larger organism that is the Yucatán which is really a land of no name.

I'm just another winged thing
Migrating back and forth
Between worlds

the spiral continues.

On a boat off the Gulf towards el ria de Celestún—Returning donde me enseño mi Xix la lengua de los flamencos y el visión del ojo del agua y la lengua de nube y sangre—Into the water again.

Even the river has changed (me)

The water is different. I think of how time uses itself as a form of paint, or covering. Now there is a bridge upon which you can walk up to see el ojo del agua y cuando yo llegue con Xix solamente había agua y raises.

I bring this up to the guide.

La última vez que visité no había ninguna plataforma ni había piso para ver el ojo de agua. Fue en puro barco que lo vimos todo. Y él me dijo: *"Es cierto, joven, mucho ha cambiado aquí y en todas partes. Hay más turistas ahora"*. That's how it seems to be, so much here has been changed by tourism which inevitably leads to an arrival departure binary, displacing the soil with the promise of globalism, and somehow the ulterior colonies are more appealing.

I've returned to the very place my family and I ate last time. I was once the sky. Even that has changed. I suppose I've changed quite a bit in 12 years. Wondering what it means to live a happy life. There are these basic questions. I am under no false pretense about reality. The reality being mortality is inevitable. I don't want to die at a company desk.

So, what does it mean to live?

It's all I have ever wanted. I didn't mean to get caught up or in so much language; I've been listening to every dream since we last spoke. I broke many promises and habits and dreams before this living got sidetracked and still I made it back to the only promise that ever mattered:

I came home.

Alive in the absence of Xix.

Soy los muertos y soy los desaparecidos y todavía estoy aquí.
Ghosts huddle into me for warmth I rest my poetry in their fire

I stopped burning things when I realized that editing praxis was
too Spanish too colonist too violent for the softness I live.

I want to read you a book of beach beneath your feet, I want to
write you here next to me so that we might breathe Celestún y
Tulum y la mar eterno, juntos.

If you speak this aloud (will you)
sew the distance between us.

I built you a house below the left nipple from which you can see
the continent sinking into the after I go.
Not a Cenote but a gulf stream. Become the sea.

Everything disintegrates into prismatic complexities of rain y
bosque

Chaac has been following me everywhere since I got here.

                                    I must be(come) the rain again.

I love the wound and how it holds me.

I meant to write "the moon," but here we are.

After an odd morning of missing dreams, we're on the road to Chichen Itza. We fly out tomorrow, or technically, I fly out on Saturday. It's hard to know how long it's been.

The largest point on my spirit quartz is missing; a jagged, rough, and beautiful absence now rests upon the crown.

I keep waking up to threads of dreams
                                                    there is never a plumb line.

       I want to see the thing for what it is. A cloud of butterflies sews the highway to the jungle as a means of reclamation. The forest slowly gathers the time to take back its distance. The vines build their own pyramids and castles. The cenotes write back and forth about their progress, counting rains until the next set of spirals. Everything is uncertain. And yet, so plainly clear.

A hole in the page appears first as a word and then a paragraph. This puncture is a type of temporal tether that is meant to open a portal.

The poem: a type of portal, punctures the vast greens all around, cupping this living language to the mouth, sipping from one another, we form a kind of song.

Now I am superfluous.

Perhaps the mosquitos gave me blood instead of taking it.

Chaac seems to follow me wherever I go. It's always raining somewhere.

In the blurry green beside me emerge giant spirits of the forest, looking like trees covered with bright green leafy vines, shining wild in the sun.

The colors grow into me; the banyan tree is just one tree.

Is my blood a type of tree?

Are you a type of flower?

Together might we blossom and become something?

I don't want to lose the square footage. I don't want to lose the angles and colors and dimensions of the house. What does it mean if the whole thing is lost and turned into concrete?

The red perimeter of what I knew will become earth once again and the last original plot of Van Nuys California will perish, what does it really matter then?

What do you know of the geographical energetic archive?

Do you understand just how much of you remains?

                                                A wild papaya falls onto the
highway

                                                  Chichen Itza emerges
beyond words.

// CHICHEN ITZA: LA CIUDAD DEL BRUJO DEL AGUA //

They won't let me climb the pyramid my ancestors built so I take a rogue stone from the central castle, hold it boldly not in pocket but palm. I remember climbing up each step holding close to thick ropes and only realizing my fear of heights once at the top. I was held by the hot green panorama unending.

There is so much less of it now; more signage; more vendors - a man carves a perfect jaguar head in 5 minutes only to pick up another formless chunk of wood and do it again. There are so many tourists I don't get a moment of peace until I sit myself down in the middle of a green field away from the pyramid.

They stopped letting people climb after the site was declared a "wonder of the world" then came the laser light shows and the advance tickets and the VIP experiences and here I am, just trying to see something these eyes had held before, but perhaps that was asking too much; perhaps I would see too much. See how the landscape has changed and dissipated, the conquests of tourists are unending. So strange how when the west says something, people listen.

I can't help but think of all the plastic I saw suffocating Yuntun; I can't help but think of the ways in which overseas investments created an artificial sand barge to hold Cancun commerce; how none of that money returns to the local economy. Once you drive far enough away from that barge it becomes panorama city and beyond that, this sentence begins to glow in the dark.

I make the following offerings to the Cenote Sagrado in silence as tourists bumble around its perimeter.

Dendritic agate carried on my person for 2.5 years.
Offered to the East.

Blue kyanite, carried on my person for 3 years.
Offered to the West.

This Cenote was robbed of its original offerings.

This sacred portal was dredged by an American anthropologist for six years until every offering was taken. I see a gleaming Frito bag floating upon the matte, adventrine green algae that covers the portal now; does anyone else make these offerings of energy and stone to Chaac anymore?

Does colonization ever end?

The shard of Chichen watches me as I move through these temporal threads; not everything written becomes woven; there's a slowed motion to the moon tonight - sometimes, everything levitates and glows.

This stone is a compass, always pointing me to what comes next.

The house is being torn down and by the time you read this, it will not exist.

"Nosotros somos la razón por la que todo está tan seguro para su familia en la tierra de tus padres."

Two cops, gripping automatic rifles, flagged us over to the side of the road, our gas tank was low—we were running on fumes hoping to make it to the next station. They asked for our identification, which we gave them. They asked if we spoke Spanish.

That's when they asked us to get out of the car.
That's when I could feel everything start to go

sideways.

They asked us if we spoke Spanish again. They asked us who we were, while holding our identification documents. They asked us what we were doing. They asked us where we were coming from. They asked us where were going.

I said we were poets.

I was there to see my family.

(Their hands steady on their rifles.)

I told them I was very poor.

I was honest with them.

One kept laughing while the other mitigated the good cop bad cop dysphoria police impose upon their prey. They kept asking things like what exactly makes one a poet and *"Oye, dime un poema, poeta. Dime un poema, si eres poeta."* The only thing my animal brain had in its memory was Macbeth's monologue, *tomorrow, and tomorrow and tomorrow creeps in petty pace from day to day* and they just laughed and laughed and wouldn't give us our identification back.

They let us know that they would be searching the car, *"abre todas las puertas."* We opened them and stood there talking about what to do. Nothing to be done. We were just waiting.

The "bad cop" (Jose Gonzales at the Mérida Check point 5:38PM I memorized this just in case it would matter someday) checked the car digging through our trash while the laughing one asked us, *"¿Cómo se dice drogas en inglés? ¿Cómo se dice alcohol en inglés? ¿Cómo se dice cerveza en inglés? ¿Por qué estás temblando?"*

Answer: (I hate the police, in any country) I said, I hadn't had enough coffee (which was also true)

They determined that we'd caused some kind of infraction/penalty that was 2,000 pesos.

We asked why and they said the rental car was missing its rear license plate (which is how the rental place gave it to me) I tried to explain, I'd left my rental papers in the place we were staying and I didn't have them on me (another infraction). *"Dime un poema si eres un poeta. Dime un poema, poeta."* Kit suggested the Macbeth monologue again, the Shakespeare ingrained in me and out it came, the doomed king of Scotts, shouting, *Out out brief candle, life is but a walking shadow, a poor player that struts his hour upon the stage*, I paraphrase full of anxious rage, the sun *it is a tale full of sound and fury told by an idiot, signifying nothing*; they asked me to translate it *"¿Y por qué estás temblando? Dime un poema. Un poema si eres poeta."*

They asked us to empty our pockets and asked if we had drugs.

We laughed.

"Mira, tenemos un médico aquí y si has fumado en los seis meses pasados, lo va a detectar." We repeated that we did not have drugs. *"¿Cómo se dice drogas en inglés? ¿Cómo se dice alcohol?"* They asked us to empty our pockets.

I had several crystals and stones with me and pulled them all out.

"¿Y esto?" one, in all seriousness, asked me, pointing to my raw kunzite, *"¿Este cristal es una droga?"* I laughed, realizing he's never seen a drug, and said, no, and proceeded to name every stone.

Esto es kunzite, y esto es garnet, y esto se llama labradorite, y estos no son drogas, son cristales.

"Ok, poeta."

They repeat the cost of our alleged infractions.

"*Dos mil pesos, poeta.*"

And suddenly bad cop pulls me aside and says, "*Oye, mira, lo podemos terminar aquí, y aquí van ser dos mil pesos,*" and he kept on with this whole, we could tow your car and you'd have to head all the way downtown to pay 2 thousand pesos, and you know, this really could be a lot worse. You're so lucky it's only this one thing and listen, "*¿Cuánto puedes pagar?*"

At this point, Kit is chatting with good cop while bad cop keeps trying to cut a deal.

"*No te quiero dejar en una mala situación. Entonces, ¿qué me puedes dar?*"

Mire, en serio, señor, soy poeta y soy pobre y no tengo dinero. El único dinero que tengo es para invitar a mis tías a comer y para gas para regresar al aeropuerto, y eso es todo lo que tengo.

"*Okay, pues dame como mil pesos.*"

Mire, señor, no tengo ni mil pesos a mi nombre.

"*Pues, mira, no te quiero dejar malo.*"

I interrupted the black box theater hellscape and said, —¿Cuánto quiere? Porque, mire, yo no quiero problemas. Solamente quiero ver a mis tías a quienes no he visto hace más de doce años. Entonces, ¿cuánto me va a cobrar por ir a ver a mi familia, señor? ¿Cuánto quiere?

"—Pues, mira, si es cien o si es mil, lo único que yo digo es que puedo llamar a los otros policías delante de ti. Les puedo dar tus placas, y ellos…"

—Señor, de verdad, ¿cuánto quiere porque no lo aguanto? Mire, éste es el único dinero que yo le puedo dar. Si yo le doy más, no voy a tener dinero para regresar. I take the bill out of my pocket and try to hand it to him; his rifle hand tenses and his free hand motions me to put it away.

"Okay pues. No aqui, hay cameras."

He finally pulls my passport out of his bullet proof vest.

"Ponlo en tu passaporte, y dame tu passaporte."

"Nosotros somos la razón por la que todo está tan seguro para su familia en la tierra de tus padres."

I do not trust the police in any country. I take my passport and slip the 200 pesos ($5) into it and bad cop completes our pointless dance. We get back into our car and head to the nearest gas station before discussing plans to find the perfect pulque which does not exist in this city.

// FINAL MORNING IN MÉRIDA //

Last night was Kit's last night here and I brought him with me to see my Tías. I've been thinking a lot about what it means to have a traveling companion become kin over the course of a journey; how chosen family emerges from unexpected turns of the spiral. How this language brings you this close to me, and how much this means despite our distances; this text glows a beacon to reach you. Y lloró puro allegria desde Cancun a Celestún hasta Mérida, until it starts raining where you're reading.

It's the last day in the land of my grandfather. The land of my ancestral bloodline (which is a spiral).

I'm a feathered serpent spiraling through the rotted corpse of history growing butterfly swarms from the exit wounds of empire.

> I suture this scar tissue with
> honey and water.

I gather roses to fill a Cenote for Kinich Ahau; I pick petals from all my organs wondering which of them will return and I might now know what it means to arrive; you'll feel it when you get here. It feels like water on earth petrichor incantations of lifting droughts from states with Chaac made sky rivers with carving earth is a kind of liquid wind; I want you to locate the soft spots near your clavicles. How might you make a little more space for spirits?

> How will your ancestors continue?

The rooster woke me this morning, bright and early, swaying in the hamaca; I made coffee. I packed my things and went out looking for Xix's house. It wasn't very far from my own two feet still too tired to do much more than park, cry, and take a foto. I put on Pedro Infante and thought of how my family would see him watering his garden singing to his roses, not noticing the passersby. I still had to see my Tía Patti y Tía Beti, Xix's only living sibling. My Tía TeTe passed away years ago; my Tía Elsie last year, and Beti is the only one left.

I went about visiting every matriarch. All the blood that remains. All who knew Xix.

Driving hundreds if not thousands of kilómetros, I drove those golden green jungles and highways and rain clouds right into my bloodstream. I learned to make a new sound out of this living.

// THE BRIGHT LIGHT THAT IS FAMILY //

Todo mi familia son místicos, sabes eso? Me entiendes mendez? Nosotros somos Maya y orgulloso de ser Maya por que somos Yucatecos and we are right here. Stop saying the Maya disappeared. Stop calling us others or aliens when the only alien to the land of turkey and deer se llamaron españoles y nos mataron. They tried to turn us to ruin and here we are, alive. I passed by so many ruins without name. I ran through the jungle crying at the lip of a Cenote before drinking its water, 140 metros across; 15 metros of depth before a darkness unknown.

El Cenote de Chuhuan made me whole.

The only Cenote of its kind between Mérida and Cancun, breathing below the surface of the earth in a limestone portal of entry. Breathing back my ancestry into me, immersed in Xibalba my blood neither blue nor red, pero, claro como el agua de un Cenote, y los caras de este tierra aparecen como flores en mi boca y mi Tía Beti me dijo que yo hablo tanto como su hermano chono (Xix still lives on in me for I am all of my ancestors).

Xix means residue in Mayataan. Y juntos somos un Xix eternal de los cosmos del mundo nuevo que estamos construyendo en el cielo.

I learned more from the heart of Xibalba than the white institutions that lent me their language and process learning words like oppression and debt. The last time I was here there was a hurricane and it seems fitting for there to be one as I depart now, madly in love con la historia de este tierra la historia de mi cultura and I would die to defend it; that's what you do for family and kin. Would you for yours?

Would you drink the spirit realm so that you would be forever tethered to them?

What would you do to pull your history out of the colonizers' fire?

Would you give it all away? Would you come home?

Are you ready to change your life now? Are you ready to reevaluate your sense of "regular reality?" Are you ready to blossom constellations from your dominant hand? Are you ready to receive the world and its unending spiral? Are you ready for your offerings dear Cenote? Are you ready to return?

There are dolphins dotting the water today. I came home to an unexpected heat, Kinich Ahau still holding onto me, I'd like to think I brought back some of the Yucatán with me. I keep thinking about writing a series of poems called "arrival studies" that never quite materializes. I write a poem in the nook of my knee and keep it there for safety. I left ahead of a solar eclipse; the peninsula called me, Chaac said, come home; it's now or never. Never did I think it would move so fast; that I would see so much. The Pacific sings itself into existence, wave and sand become particle only to turn into words. Birds dive offshore as the dolphins dissipate to their beautiful mysteries in the deepening(rising) sea.

The sublime can often take you by surprise while eating salsa that summons your ancestors, returning memories from the void beyond spiral, safeguarded for the better part of a decade. The hospital, everyone shadowed; mourning in my memory, the architecture grown vague.

I'm a lot less hungry for distance since returning. After making my offerings I found Kinich Ahau had kissed my right wrist and the semicircles of the solar eclipse were pressed into my skin, forming a small galaxy of memory in the body. Highways pressed into my biology, there's an airplane overhead and I don't know that we appreciate the miracle of flight as much as we should this mechanical ability to fold time in the atmosphere.

To become enmeshed with the cloud net. To sew the sky to the earth and back again, walking back and forth above the clouds for circulation; the calming clarity of cabin pressure: the acceptance that you might die amongst complete strangers, reduced to axons and dendrites firing against the color of oblivion. You'll have to let go.

You have to give yourself over to another form of living where you are grateful for the(se) moment; at this very moment, right now, you are alive. Your body is an airplane. You shepherd many spirits because you are such an abundance of energy and language.

You are a miracle.

May you always arrive to where you're going.

I'll see you there soon, dear one.

El sonámbulx se llena con palabras y lenguas y empieza mover sus alas y sus pies y la ciudad empieza llorar. Los sueños pueden cambiar tu vida. La vida no se suelta sin querer pedirse. Me voy a desaparecer en estas palabras. Me voy a quedar aquí contigo hasta que estés viejitx porque somos árboles de sonido y tiempo. Nunca somos solos porque hablamos con la tierra y cantamos con la Lluvia. Cuando estamos cerca el planeta empieza su baile con la luna; los pájaros se suben al techo y juntos los ayudamos a salvar la casa y la huerta —que los guardan entre el polvo de la luna—. Aquí podemos empezar otra vez, sin ciudad ni nación, y sin los hilos de mala suerte que comieron la calle. Ya veo que no fue posible a salvar la casa. Sé que no puedo salvar la ciudad. No puedo salvar la huerta. Pero, yo me acuerdo. Y las memorias son como la Lluvia en que nunca se olvida nada y es así como continuamos, cerca del mar y llenos con los sueños atómicos que dan vida a los espíritus que andan cansados como yo y siempre luchando con el sol; luchando con el estado y luchando para vivir libres. Y estos sonámbulxs son mi familia, como mi propia familia de sangre. Somos soñadorxs y nos comunicamos sin conceptos como tiempo y espacio porque entendemos que la vida es otro tipo de sueño y queremos que todxs sean felices con su tiempo sobre este planeta raro. No quiero que te olvides de que no necesitamos al estado para soñar; pero sí descanso y esperanza. Tus sueños —mi cariño, mi familia— son un tipo de medicina para la enfermedad del capitalismo, que borró el sueño de la casa y la ciudad. Y todavía ando buscando repuestas en los siglos después de mi muerte. Tú, mi sonámbula, ¿cuándo eres? ¿A dónde te vas? Y lo más importante: ¿qué vas a hacer ahora que sabes que los sueños, igual que las lenguas que habitas, existen para cambiar tu realidad?

How do we mourn a space, or location, differently than we mourn the dead? What does it mean to lose one's constant space of return/arrival?

There are times when writing where I feel the fold of time and space. This temporal collapse gives me a sense of hope beyond history as history;

"We have poetry so that we might survive history."
                                                    - Meena Alexander

This is a kind of living notebook.
This is a kind of Now that folds.

Which is to say:

A book is a kind of port of entry that contracts or expands; a book is an ongoing conversation; we pick up another set of neurons, we pick up another living; we become another organism by reading, expanding this reality to fit, another. The dream here (as always) is a blur of the (in)betweenness that separates us.

The house in your heart burns down from the unattended candle. You try to hold onto light like cupping the ocean in your palms; everything is a kind of spillage, or excess. The house is saved only by the rain you produce once you realize the wreckage is not an image but an actuality.

> Grief is a finicky ocean,
> > no matter how you approach it.

You begin construction on a new house within your body; you find a patch of time to plant this projection into the future. Someday, you may live there when the earth grows quiet. This time the fire won't leave.

Sometimes I forget to think about that book as a kind of coping/memory-retention method; I don't know what it really is, but now that I'm older, I return to those rooms and airports with the candles still lit; the lights on and the lines longer. There are more blue hews than before. The airport is older and filled with more creatures waiting to connect and return and arrive.

I've been avoiding a lot of architectures that exist upon the continent I created in my body; these structures will not fail.

What is a book? What is it for?

What happens when the very book you're writing after is in fact a failure. I said nothing for so long and woke up muttering. I re-open the line in my thigh until another map emerges. I press this entryway against a pair of glass slides, and slowly another continent emerges.

I plant the orchard atop a mountain and suddenly a runway strip emerges beside the anomalous tract of land; a splintering of temporal pockets begins to refract the various nervous systems encountering the space. The nervous system pulsates with recognition.

I build these nests of language to hide in; I keep crafting these disposable architectures, cast out ephemeral honey tones. The pulsations of sound and image are meant to resonate as much as they dispel.

Do you want to know a secret?

This all began with a dream between Spain and San Jose. This all began with a dream. The word is ongoing, beyond the vessel - thought become breath become energy again. Time collapses in all directions during the reading of a sentence, or a line of poetry. The harmonies contained within the resonance are what bridges time and space. The vibrations of language call us together to change our energy.

A language of crystals and stones and sun and road and rain and.

There is no capturing of the moment.

                              The moment supersedes you.

There is no capturing the moment.

The city is a kind of sky, as are you as am I and

the vibrations of language call us together to (ex)change energies.

The harmonies contained within the resonance are what bridges time and space.

Language like a spell.

The word is ongoing, beyond every flesh vessel - thought becomes breath becomes energy again until there's nothing there anymore.

The night continues and the insomnia returns. The moon is a vibrant crescent cutting through the thick veil of vacuum and sky. The gardenias won't grow but they won't die either. The lemons began fruiting, the rain wouldn't stop for several days; waterfalls and atmospheric rivers emerged. The mountain covered in a nest of rain. The air forms a frequency. The sleep continues to elude the somnambulist and it's unclear whether the butterfly or the human is dreaming; both must surely be tired. The valley turns viscous during the flights that do and do not happen; a chrysalis of distance begins to enmesh the city from foothill to flatland to beach and beyond; the whole city breaks down mercurial and rests behind the borders of time and space and the city is hard at work the whole time through.

There is no home to return to. The geography inevitably turns to rubble; the seas become vertical stone with enough time. We live upon a lot of time. A lot of language. A lot of suffering. A whole of change.

Time is fickle that way. Dreams, too. Sometimes we forget the intensity of the other realities we sleep through; they send breadcrumbs and clues through the day to spark a moment of recall in which these realities are coexistent.

We dredge through the whole of history to emerge tomorrow, alive or dead. Are you still there? Do you ever feel the spectrum of other timelines pull at you? Do you remember your dreams now, more than before?

What do you place between the book and yourself?

The city in my dreams is not my city but the way I keep my city alive in my mind's eye; in the city of my dreams the orchard remains untouched; still standing. The city I grew up in does not exist, nor has it ever. Cities are constant and unraveling, not fixed and yet immovable.

There's a minutia at work across the spectrum of light I experience; maybe you've seen it too: the tug of the way things could (have) be(en); how the ancillary realities splinter moments so easily. What if you had answered your phone, or left a few minutes later; what if you didn't sign your name or didn't leave or what if you kept becoming?

The resonance is part sunlight by which I mean mostly moon. The mirror made of earth rib only earth is all mothers. To have vacated the time stream. Having only half read things there comes another way of seeing by feeling. Energetic osmosis by proxy we might be folding time in this small moment of language and breathing.

In the after of it all time fluctuates across multiplicities of reality. Sometimes we slide into other dimensions daydreaming as we murk down the highway not pummeling but tunneling forward through time and geography. Some days I wonder what the sky thinks about me. I worry that the clouds feel too heavy to themselves and I wonder if the sun has anxiety. I'm always in a rain it seems. Seems I am so much highway and forgetting. Sometimes I feel obvious. Sometimes I find the salt in the air and know where the ocean will go. I had to leave the mountains to find myself again. On the orchard time moves differently. The cactus turns to goo under the abundance of rain. Then there's the camellias again. There's that mirror again - positioning language in such a way that our temporal dissonance finds its harmonies. I need you to sing with me. I need you to believe me. We can fold this temporal tract and you can sit next to me on this bus as we carve out the edge of a continent. Hold me down like language holds rain; these words eat each other and we breathe when we need to. Language is ever emergent; mercurial - the whole sequence like a static in the waves.

Celestún shimmers in my breathing. I pour a pound of salt out of my eyeballs and exhale 12 miles of sand for you to walk along. I am always this much beach. I am always this space. Even when I'm working. Even when I'm crying. Even when I'm alone. I am cosmic imprint heavy with the memory of that which ails me. That which I have failed to do.

In my dreams I drive from here to Mérida. I drive from here to 2006. I drive from here to where you are now. We form a new language from our distant dissonance. I'm never on time.

A Cenote opens up to eat the house. To keep it safe.
    The house is with the ancestors now.

The inhabitants scatter across the city void and beyond. The pitaya becomes several palms around the city. The roses explode out across the landscape blossoming in the rain before evaporating along with the water. The aguacates lend themselves to immigrant households to keep their families fed. The lemons scatter along with the oranges to form two new tints of sunlight that always look like Mama's lemons and Xix's oranges.

The colors of the house become other times of day lilting memories from the soul of those who know how precious this dream can be. I tattoo the wallpaper to my body. I dig a hole where I keep every stone safe. The house itself evaporates into a rain that does not end by which I mean all our dreams become clouds to nourish the future. To nourish our ancestors and those who are gone, but still roaming with(in) us.

I have a dream where I drive the entirety of the grid while the city sleeps. I work the city's sleep into a type of fabric to craft a shawl. Quiero hacer una tilma de Los Ángeles y el poder de sus sueños. No me quiero olvidar de nada cuando llega el tiempo a soñar otro sueño. Quiero ser como un hilo de luz. A costurar los sueños los vidas los tiempos. No quiero que nadien se olvida. Somos flores que cresan a manifestar lo que nunca a pasado antes.

There are more words right now than there have ever been before.

I think eventually I'll learn to let go of the city.

Or I will become the City. There is no in between.
Mérida melts into the mountain, or as the clouds skim the microclimate, the image of the peninsula drizzles, made prismatic by the morning sunlight.

It's in these moments I see you most clearly. When the sky opens up its portals. When the light leans into you.

We converse in these moments of liminality; our language is a strong light that guides spirits home beyond the structure of a house. Light a candle tonight with the intention of hope beyond hope. Leave it burning until the wax has ended its verticality. What do you see

when this now becomes before?
In the valley of your spine lies a harvest of endocrine flowers that give you a new, soft life.

You tend to them by taking it easy on yourself; learning to cry; returning to write; writing this book together, right now.

I dreamt we wrote that.

I keep nodding off into the spiral. Like 6am finger tips touching a stream both frozen and running; there is a continuity to the way these electrons hummmm.

The swaying of the pen keeps reversing its order forming other portals and words I don't know. The rain taps at your window in triplets on the bus or airplane; the atmosphere grows a language to understand itself.

As the house is destroyed its components become dispersed across the city; ten thousand palm trees become stories for pitayas to assemble, blossoming in the moonlight and giving others a language; we water them with it. The bricks replace other bricks across the city on both sides of the hill forming a nexus of echoic memory. In the moment of oblivion, three crops of avocados instantly withered in the hands of the gentry; they could only taste battery acid and earth. The flowers floated themselves into clouds and brought rain down through the grid of territory.

At the end of the orchard, nothing makes as much sense as when the orchard appeared beside the lone airstrip in the redwood forest, which itself was an opaque dream bereft of waking logic.

The trees grow smaller as the plot of earth begins to swirl, slow as the solstice sun – the structures unmake themselves and the boards of the homes become trees unpainted, not-nailed; the architectural components rejoin the un-angled shapes of the soil. The acreage tips over into the ravine only to remain suspended between the spiral of soil and sky – the language lingering between your lungs and mouth.

What changes when you speak these spells aloud?

How will you go on living now?

What, if anything has changed?

How will you change?

What will you grow (into)?

Who will you continue becoming?

Time to (wake up and) get to it.

ENDNOTES

1. *A note on the opening poem* (p.11). This is my Grandmother's poem which was written in Spanish. I've decided to keep it this way without translation because these are her words, and this is not a book about translation so much as it is a multilingual/translingual text. It didn't feel right to translate her poem.

2. *A note on the following prose block* (p. 12). The following prose block that appears after the poem is similarly not translated because it's a continuation of my grandmother's poem and in many ways, it's a letter to my grandmother with whom I solely communicate in Spanish. It felt wrong to translate this language which seeks to continue the language of my grandmother both in energy and in tongue. The rest of the untranslated Spanish throughout the book stands as an invitation to decentralize our notions of linguistic supremacy, asking non-Spanish speaking readers to do a bit of "extra work" if they wish to gain entrance into the language concealed therein. At the same time, this is also an invitation for Spanish-speakers, to hopefully see themselves refracted in these moments of Spanish without translation. It's my hope that this resistance to translation acts as an invitation to activation.

ACKNOWLEGEMENTS

Special thanks is owed to Elae whose commitment and vision of the OS continues to inspire and instruct; grateful that you believed in me, and the possibilities of this writing. Thank you for putting up with and understanding the process behind this Cenote of language. Eternally grateful for all that you do!

Eternal thanks are owed to my entire family who have held space for me since the moment I came into existence in this reality. Especially Mamá (Sofia Dominguez), Xix (Jose Asunción Dominguez), Joe (Jose Martin Hipolito Dominguez Sanchez); Danny (Cosme D. Dominguez); Gab (Sofia Dominguez) and my mom (Yazmin Dominguez de Sanchez). It was all of you who raised me after all.

Gracias a todo mi familia en el Yucatán. Gracias a la familia Burgos. Gracias a la familia Dominguez. Gracias a Magui, Miriam, Thely, Patricia, Beatriz, Yolanda, Daniela, y Israel. Los quiero mucho. Esté libro también es para mi Tío Pepe y Mi Tía Elsy. Love to my siblings who I look up to and who continue to inspire me everyday. Gustavo, Olivia, Alejandro, and Daniel. Don't stop dreaming.

Special thanks to the homies who were there for me during the writing of this book and who encouraged me to press on even when I wanted to quit. Daniel Talamantes; Raquel Salas Rivera; Kristen E. Nelson; Eric Sneathen; Domingo Canizales III; Ivy Johnson; Jamie Townsend; Paul Ebenkamp; DJ Jebejian; Alex Weinschenker (memory eternal); Erick Sáenz; Josh Brodey; Jack Goode; MJ Malpiedi; Kit Schluter, dearest Kin. Gracias to Patricia Arredondo for all your help with grammar! Thank you to Ronaldo V. Wilson who continues to offer transformative energy to my life. Thank you to my students at CSUMB (2017-19) who that taught me a great deal about the power of writing.

My deepest thanks and appreciation to Brenda Iijima, Lara Mimosa Montes, Gabriel Ojeda-Sagué, and Tatiana Luboviski-Acosta, for your shining brilliance, and for taking the time to blurb this wily wild tongue in process. Your words helped me see everything more clearly. Your writing changed and continues to change my life, and I'm grateful for all of you. A special thanks to Sesshu Foster, for telling me I was a poet all those years ago, for believing in me and my writing, and setting me on this path.

Grateful to the editors and places that published various pieces in various phases of revision, especially *Amerarcana no. 8; The Spectacle Magazine; Small Press Traffic*.

Love to Hannah who continues to teach me about being alive. Love to Luna our Little cat, who encouraged many early morning hours of edits and rewrites.

Love to the land itself,
Love to anyone I forgot to mention here,
and: Love to you, dearest reader. Thank you for this exchange of energies.
Till next time ;)

The size and scale of the book was determined through a somatic ritual that involved the author moving through their bookshelves in a kind of bibliomancy focused on the tactile experience of the work. This was further considered against the original notebooks that contain some of the writing that appears within the text itself – the notebook being, about the size of this book. The cover font [Albion] was selected for its familial resonances and energetic embodiment of the author's Latinx experience growing up in Los Angeles, CA. The writing itself originally appeared as a more compact reservoir of writing that was widened by Elæ during an operating system meeting with Brent Armendinger. It was during this meeting that the author realized just how much more held by the widened prose blocks they felt, seeing how this widened form lent itself to the original intentions of creating a "Dzonot/Cenote" form, acting as a kind of groundwater system of language and energy. The hope is for the reader to experience these reservoirs of energy, lived experience, and refracted memory as though swimming, or traveling through between these realms of thought, connected by the experience of reading.

The interior body font of this volume is Minion Pro, with titles in FreightNeo Pro Book, at 10 pt., and the book itself is sized at 6" x 9."

The digital form allows for the book to exist in ways that are perhaps not possible for the physical book. It further allows a kind of "free dive" into the text for readers to scroll/scan/zoom/engage with as they wish. It also keeps the energies within the writing available beyond physical means, allowing for a kind of unique immediacy to the text.

At this time this book does not yet exist in other media forms. There are currently plans to record an audio version of the book as read by the author which will hopefully have accompanying visual video materials that will be accessible online. This extension of the text is still in process.

LUMINOUS NOURISHMENT:
THE LIVING CENOTE OF LANGUAGE

An OS [re:con]versation with Angel Dominguez

Greetings comrade! Thank you for talking to us about your process today! Can you introduce yourself, in a way that you would choose?

Angel Dominguez, Latinx smudge of spirit and flesh, blessed to still be alive in this very moment moving through this reality, ever onwards. Born in Los Angeles, raised by my entire Yucateco immigrant family from Hollywood to Van Nuys. Oldest of 5. Driver of many highways; lover of tacos.

Why are you a poet/writer/artist?

I have no choice in the matter. It's what I do. What I am. Every waking moment is language and poetry; I've been stubborn in this way, stealing time from capitalist entanglements and always placing poetry and writing and making at the forefront of my consciousness. I listen to the things my dreams tell me; the words that make it through the static of the quotidian.

When did you decide you were a poet/writer/artist (and/or: do you feel comfortable calling yourself a poet/writer/artist, what other titles or affiliations do you prefer/ feel are more accurate)?

I can actually tell you the moment when I finally thought of myself as being considered a poet. It was 2010; my life was falling apart (some things never change) and I was just failing at everything, I was living alone in Bonny Doon without a car and riding my bike down a mountain every day for class (something I would later try when moving back here only to realize that I no longer had the sense of invincibility I once had in my youth and never tried it again) – I was absolutely fucking up my "second chance" at "going to college," but I was writing every single day. The one class that meant the most to me was Sesshu Foster's intermediate poetry class at UCSC. I learned so much there and made it a point to always go to his office hours to talk to him. One particularly awful week, I went into his office and proceeded to lay out the ways in which my life was falling apart, and he, being the knowing, wise poet he is, leaned back in his chair, looked at me, and said, "you know, those sound like poet problems." And I don't think I ever considered myself a poet before that moment in time. It felt like I'd earned something I'd felt all along. Like hearing it aloud allowed me to accept myself. Being a poet/writer/artist isn't something you decide so much as something you are. I don't know. If you know you know. And if you know, it's over for you. You've got to do the thing.

What's a "poet" (or "writer" or "artist") anyway? What do you see as your cultural and social role (in the literary / artistic / creative community and beyond)?

A poet is more than I could put language to; I think that's the sort of low down truth to the whole thing: the poet is an animal of consciousness compressing these tracts of experience and thought into language. The poet is here to act as a channel between the divine/source/universe/cosmos and spoken. To bring a kind of tangibility to the ineffable in language, creating these temporary autonomous zones of possibility. The poet is here to do what is called of them. To document typically undocumented histories and existences. Always in favor of the collective whole; always in service of the people. The deeply personal may be universal. Poets are here to help. And if you're not here to help in some way. You're not a poet. I always think of what Amiri Baraka said during a lecture at Naropa University back in the summer of 2013, It's always stayed with me: "If you're not ready to go do the work, don't be a poet. Go do something soft."

Talk about the process or instinct to move these poems (or your work in general) as independent entities into a body of work. How and why did this happen? Have you had this intention for a while? What encouraged and/or confounded this (or a book, in general) coming together? Was it a struggle?

In the making of this book of writing which can be read as a book of poems or a kind of phenomenological travelogue of the interior experiencing the exterior journey. It's a language written out of a frenzied exhaustion. Much of the "Yucatan" writing emerged from the energies of the earth itself, language emerged from Tulum, Yuntun, Valladolid, Merida, Celestun, Los Angeles, and everything in between.

The process of these poems, this language, was a matter of return; a long awaited arrival to a future that was never guaranteed. I'll be very honest with you. The only reason I could even afford to go on that trip is because I was part of a union that won a contract negotiation against a university that continues to negotiate the quality of life it chooses to provide to their workers (and student workers), knowing full well it could eliminate the private police budget it has on campus in order to give their grad students enough to live, but that's another story for another time. I've been poor all my life and I never thought I'd actually get the chance to return to the Yucatan; that's why my first book was about a flight that never happened; it was never supposed to happen. And it did.

I should also say that around this time I was working a job that was absolutely soul-crushing in every way. So much so, I wasn't able to write for months and months, and I think it had been a full year since I'd written something that meant something to me prior to the trip. Once I left the country, it's like a faucet opened up. I spent the entire trip writing. I filled up an entire notebook.

Then I was working full time in Santa Cruz and teaching in Monterey; that's when I learned the house was being sold. This book took everything to come together. The house I wrote about was quite literally destroyed; my grandmother tells me that there are apartments or condos there now. I can't bring myself to drive down that street anymore. In the final year of the manuscript, I encountered a bear on a hike in Yosemite; evacuated my home and was displaced for a month because of the CZU lightning complex fires and in this final month of the never ending year that is 2020, my sister contracted covid-19 as I was trying to finish the final edits for the manuscript. I'm so thankful that she's alive and recovering.

Did you envision this collection as a collection or understand your process as writing or making specifically around a theme while the poems themselves were being written / the work was being made? How or how not?

I think what this book is/became is not necessarily how/what I "envisioned." When I started writing again after a long drought of not being able to write anything, there was a familiarity to the voice of the writing. It was a voice I thought I'd buried – there was an echoic kinship to the energy of that writing that recalled *Black Lavender Milk*, and yet it was also doing something else I didn't quite understand. This book was something else entirely and then I helped my grandmother pack up the family home, driving back and forth from Bonny Doon to Van Nuys every weekend for two months. During that time, she found an old poem that she had written; it was the first I'd ever heard of her writing poetry. It's the first poem that appears in this book, it stuck with me and caused me to shift the trajectory of the writing. Or rather, the writing that was occurring during this time was energetically tethered to the Yucatan writing. I believe in trusting the writing over everything – the writing knows more than the writer does. This is what I mean in terms of a bioluminescent writing: it's a kind of energetic eminence that acts a signal or magnet. It calls out to the poet/writer who does their best to adorn the ineffable with language. It's in that way this book brought itself together, out of the rubble of its many variant trajectories.

What formal structures or other constrictive practices (if any) do you use in the creation of your work? Have certain teachers or instructive environments, or readings/writings/work of other creative people informed the way you work/write?

In terms of formal structures, this writing takes on a self imposed marginal constraint meant to embody a Cenote (Dzonot is actually the indigenous spelling of the word, however the most common spelling is in Spanish, so for clarity sake, I've opted for the Spanish spelling throughout the text) form/feeling. The Cenote which is a kind of portal to Xibalba, the Yucatec Maya underworld. These limestone caverns go out for miles and are interconnected through various currents and labyrinthine tunnels and passages which eventually reach the saltwater of the seas surrounding the peninsula. The entire poem (I meant to write book, but perhaps the subconscious knows better than I) emerges from the cavernous stanzas of my grandmother's language; there is a wider portal carved out of my own language, and various chambers of language proceed. This self-imposed "Cenote-form" of marginal constriction holds the intention of crafting kind of living cenote of language – this channel of energy and nourishment made possible by language; these pools and chambers of feeling, writing, thinking, and being, becoming actualized in this kind of subterranean concentration of intention and sound. When talking with Elæ over a video call and going over the layout for the book, they adjusted the margins to be a bit wider than the original manuscript. I felt so held by these wider prose blocks, somehow more invited to stay within, and move through the language contained. It was obvious that it had to be this way.

The geographic energies of the Yucatan Peninsula, my Grandmother's house in Van Nuys, the redwood forest of Santa Cruz; all these things have further influenced the writing in ways I can't quite put a language to. Places hold power. You feel it when you're there. There's this sensation of maybe pressure, or warmth in your chest. You can notice how you're breathing differently, or perhaps you've just been made more aware of it by the earth that holds you in place. This writing is very much a consequence of the spaces in which it emerged.

This writing comes from living. I think a lot about what that means: writing to live. Not as a means to a capitalistic end (e.g. writing full time to pay the bills), but more so as a means of moving through the world and reporting back these warbling field notes, live from the eye(s) of existence.

Speaking of monikers, what does your title represent? How was it generated? Talk about the way you titled the book, and how your process of naming (individual pieces, sections, etc) influences you and/or colors your work specifically.

Rose Sun Water was always going to be the title. It came to me while on that trip to the Yucatan. The image of it. Like water trapped in rose quartz being held up to the sun. The feeling of that. When arriving to Chichen Itza. When watching the sun rise over Celestun. It's what I remember most about my grandmother's home. A space that no longer exists as of the publication of this book. The roses. The sun. The water. This text hopes to hold the feeling of that, the mourning of a space; the growing beyond that. The "positive disintegration" making way for what comes next.As for the sections, many if not all the names come directly from the notebooks from which they were culled.

What does this particular work represent to you as indicative of your method/ creative practice? your history, your mission, intentions, hopes and/or plans?

[This] writing is a refuge for all who seek it. This menagerie of dreams; memories; rumination, and possibility through poetry is a love letter to the constantly under-construction city I'm from; it's a letter of love, hope, and resilience to my kin, not just family, but the kin whose nervous systems are activated to action by the language of the text. **RSW** is a whole continent of my history, my body, life; living. It's a mode of resistance against gentrification, this attempt at documenting invisible histories. This book is an ode to a home that was swallowed up by the ever changing face of the city I love, the city I'm from. It's also a deep meditation on writing, and what writing is or means in relation to the experience of being alive; how we might be able to transmit not simply language and ideas, but energy through writing. The activation of nervous systems and mirror neurons. I think that's the real hope of this work.

What does this book DO (as much as what it says or contains)?

Whether or not this book "does" anything is entirely up to (you) the reader – I sincerely hope this book does, what I think all great works do, and that's the invocation of feeling. I hope this book activates as much as it illuminates or resonates. Maybe you dear reader are on a kind of journey or quest back to who you are, or who you might become; perhaps you needed a little nudge of luminescent resonance, a sign that you're on the right path. Maybe you need(ed) a space to remember, or retrieve dream energies; a space to rest and recuperate. I hope this book is that.

What would be the best possible outcome for this book? What might it do in the world, and how will its presence as an object facilitate your creative role in your community and beyond? What are your hopes for this book, and for your practice?

I hope this book, as with all my writing, helps in some small way. I don't know, I've never read a book about Van Nuys and maybe that's on me, but I hope readers are able to see themselves in this writing. Selfishly, I hope this book helps my family heal. I think we're all in need of healing and I honestly do believe that engaging with writing, whether reading or writing, can be healing. May this book move forward through time like a Pitaya growing up a palm tree, blooming with every full moon and gathering luminosity.

I also hope this text makes its reader think about what all these acts of reading and writing might mean and how we are connected to one another through energy and lineage in ways that supersede chronology or geographical proximity. I hope even just one one line of this text meant something to you. I hope it moves forward with you wherever you're going.

Let's talk a little bit about the role of poetics and creative community in social and political activism, so present in our daily lives as we face the often sobering, sometimes dangerous realities of the Capitalocene. How does your process, practice, or work otherwise interface with these conditions?

I'll say this: my life in some ways, is lived entirely out of spite. I don't know that I separate my life from my creative practice. Everything is the project, or works towards the project, or the next project. Life is always happening. In process. Poetry is inherently anti-capitalist because it makes you stop and think. It slows production. Poetry is a craft as much as it is a kind of living. It can keep you living. I have a lot of complicated feelings about community and tend to think more in terms of homies, kin, and accomplices. We help keep one another safe and surviving.

I'd be curious to hear some of your thoughts on the challenges we face in speaking and publishing across lines of race, age, ability, class, privilege, social/cultural background, gender, sexuality (and other identifiers) within the community as well as creating and maintaining safe spaces, vs. the dangers of remaining and producing in isolated "silos" and/or disciplinary and/or institutional bounds?

I feel like you could fill a whole other book answering this question, so I'll say this.

May we all do what we can to meet these challenges in ways that promote a sense of growth rather than replication. Everyone deserves access to the tools necessary to achieve liberation. The time of gatekeepers and exclusory communities attempting to hoard the aforementioned tools has long been up. Connect with your kin and remain vigilant. May we all live long enough to see our enemies fall.

Is there anything else we should have asked, or that you want to share?

End Policing. Abolish prisons. Land back. Global Reparations.
Abolish billionaires & millionaires. End gentrification.

Shout out Van Nuys, the gr818. While they may gentrify your body, may they never gentrify your soul!

And you, dearest reader. Don't Panic. Keep at it. Never Give Up. Fear not.

Love you forever.

The author and their grandmother Sofía Domínguez in front of the Van Nuys house before it was torn down

ANGEL DOMINGUEZ is a Latinx poet and artist of Yucatec Maya descent, born in Hollywood and raised in Van Nuys, CA by their immigrant family. They're the author of *ROSESUNWATER* (The Operating System, 2021) and *Black Lavender Milk* (Timeless, Infinite Light 2015). Angel earned a BA from the University of California Santa Cruz and an MFA from the Jack Kerouac School of Disembodied Poetics at Naropa University in Boulder Colorado. You can find Angel's work online and in print in various publications. You can find Angel in the redwoods or ocean. Their third book, *DESGRACIADO* (the collected letters) is forthcoming with Nightboat Books in 2022.

ABOUT GLOSSARIUM : UNSILENCED TEXTS

The Operating System's GLOSSARIUM: UNSILENCED TEXTS series was established in early 2016 in an effort to recover silenced voices outside and beyond the canon, seeking out and publishing contemporary translations, translingual projects, and little or un-known out of print texts, in particular those under siege by restrictive regimes and silencing practices in their home (or adoptive) countries. We are committed to producing dual-language versions whenever possible.

Few, even avid readers, are aware of the startling statistic reporting that less than three percent of all books published in the United States, per UNESCO, are works in translation. Less than one percent of these (closer to 0.7%) are works of poetry and fiction. You can imagine that even less of these are experimental or radical works, in particular those from countries in conflict with the US or where funding is hard to come by.

Other countries are far, far ahead of us in reading and promoting international literature, a trend we should be both aware of and concerned about—how does it come to pass that attentions in the US become so myopic, and as a result, so under-informed? We see the publication of translations, especially in volume, to be a vital and necessary act for all publishers to require of themselves in the service of a more humane, globally aware, world. By publishing 7 titles in 2019, we raised the number of translated books of literature published in the US that year *by a full percent*. We plan to continue this growth as much as possible.

The dual-language and translingual titles either in active circulation or forthcoming in this series include Arabic-English, Farsi-English, Polish-English, French-English, Faroese-English, German-English, Danish-English, Yaqui Indigenous American translations, Yiddish-English and Spanish-English translations from Cuba, Argentina, Mexico, Uruguay, Bolivia, and Puerto Rico.

The term 'Glossarium' derives from latin/greek and is defined as 'a collection of glosses or explanations of words, especially of words not in general use, as those of a dialect, locality or an art or science, or of particular words used by an old or a foreign author.' The series is curated by OS Founder and Creative Director Elæ with the help of global collaborators and friends.

ABOUT KIN(D)* TEXTS & PROJECTS

RoseSunWater is a simultaneous publication under the OS & Liminal Lab's KIN(D)* imprint, a dedication to continuously publishing the work of trans and gender nonconforming creative practitioners.

The Operating System uses the language "print document" to differentiate from the book-object as part of our mission to distinguish the act of documentation-in-book-FORM from the act of publishing as a backwards-facing replication of the book's agentive *role* as it may have appeared the last several centuries of its history. Ultimately, I approach the book as TECHNOLOGY: one of a variety of printed documents (in this case, bound) that humans have invented and in turn used to archive and disseminate ideas, beliefs, stories, and other evidence of production.

Ownership and use of printing presses and access to (or restriction of printed materials) has long been a site of struggle, related in many ways to revolutionary activity and the fight for civil rights and free speech all over the world. While (in many countries) the contemporary quotidian landscape has indeed drastically shifted in its access to platforms for sharing information and in the widespread ability to "publish" digitally, even with extremely limited resources, the importance of publication on physical media has not diminished. In fact, this may be the most critical time in recent history for activist groups, artists, and others to insist upon learning, establishing, and encouraging personal and community documentation practices. Hear me out.

With The OS's print endeavors I wanted to open up a conversation about this: the ultimately radical, transgressive act of creating PRINT / DOCUMENTATION in the digital age. It's a question of the archive, and of history: who gets to tell the story, and what evidence of our life, our behaviors, our experiences are we leaving behind? We can know little to nothing about the future into which we're leaving an unprecedentedly digital document trail — but we can be assured that publications, government agencies, museums, schools, and other institutional powers that be will continue to leave BOTH a digital and print version of their production for the official record. Will we?

As a (rogue) anthropologist and long time academic, I can easily pull up many accounts about how lives, behaviors, experiences — how THE STORY of a time or place — was pieced together using the deep study of correspondence, notebooks, and other physical documents which are no longer the norm in many lives and practices. As we move our creative behaviors towards digital note taking, and even audio and video, what can we predict about future technology that is in any way assuring that our stories will be accurately told – or told at all? How will we leave these things for the record? In these documents we say:

WE WERE HERE, WE EXISTED, WE HAVE A DIFFERENT STORY

- Elæ [Lynne DeSilva-Johnson], Founder/Creative Director

2020-21

Institution is a Verb: A Panoply Performance Lab Compilation
Vidhu Aggarwal - Daughter Isotope
Johnny Damm - Failure Biographies
Power ON - Ginger Ko
Spite - Danielle Pafunda
Acid Western - Robert Balun

KIN(D)* TEXTS AND PROJECTS

Intergalactic Travels: Poems from a Fugutive Alien - Alan Pelaez Lopez
HOAX - Joey De Jesus [Kin(d)*]
RoseSunWater - Angel Dominguez [Kin(d)*/Glossarium]

GLOSSARIUM: UNSILENCED TEXTS AND TRANSLATIONS

Between Language and Justice: Selected Writings from Antena Aire
(Jen Hofer & John Pluecker))
Steven Alvarez - Manhatitlán [Glossarium]
Híkurí (Peyote) - José Vincente Anaya (tr. Joshua Pollock)
Ernst Toller's "Vormorgen" & Emmy Hennings - Radical Archival Translations -
Mathilda Cullen [Glossarium x Kin(d)*; German-English]
Black and Blue Partition ('Mistry) - Monchoachi (tr. Patricia Hartland)
[Glossarium; French & Antillean Creole/English]

IN CORPORE SANO

Hypermobilities - Ellen Samuels
Goodbye Wolf-Nik DeDominic

2019

Ark Hive-Marthe Reed
I Made for You a New Machine and All it Does is Hope - Richard Lucyshyn
Illusory Borders-Heidi Reszies
A Year of Misreading the Wildcats - Orchid Tierney
Of Color: Poets' Ways of Making | An Anthology of Essays on
Transformative Poetics - Amanda Galvan Huynh & Luisa A. Igloria, Editors

KIN(D)* TEXTS AND PROJECTS

A Bony Framework for the Tangible Universe-D. Allen [In Corpore Sano]
Opera on TV-James Brunton
Hall of Waters-Berry Grass
Transitional Object-Adrian Silbernagel

GLOSSARIUM: UNSILENCED TEXTS AND TRANSLATIONS

Śnienie / Dreaming - Marta Zelwan/Krystyna Sakowicz,
(Poland, trans. Victoria Miluch)
High Tide Of The Eyes - Bijan Elahi (Farsi-English/dual-language)
trans. Rebecca Ruth Gould and Kayvan Tahmasebian
In the Drying Shed of Souls: Poetry from Cuba's Generation Zero
Katherine Hedeen and Víctor Rodríguez Núñez, translators/editors
Street Gloss - Brent Armendinger with translations of Alejandro Méndez,
Mercedes Roffé, Fabián Casas, Diana Bellessi
& Néstor Perlongher (Argentina)
Operation on a Malignant Body - Sergio Loo
(Mexico, trans. Will Stockton)[In Corpore Sano]
Are There Copper Pipes in Heaven - Katrin Ottarsdóttir
(Faroe Islands, trans. Matthew Landrum)

DOC U MENT
/däkyəmənt/

First meant "instruction" or "evidence," whether written or not.

noun - a piece of written, printed, or electronic matter that provides information or evidence or that serves as an official record *verb* - record (something) in written, photographic, or other form *synonyms* - paper - deed - record - writing - act - instrument

[*Middle English, precept, from Old French, from Latin documentum, example, proof, from docre, to teach; see dek- in Indo-European roots.*]

Who is responsible for the manufacture of value?

Based on what supercilious ontology have we landed in a space where we vie against other creative people in vain pursuit of the fleeting credibilities of the scarcity economy, rather than freely collaborating and sharing openly with each other in ecstatic celebration of MAKING?

While we understand and acknowledge the economic pressures and fear-mongering that threatens to dominate and crush the creative impulse, we also believe that ***now more than ever we have the tools to redistribute agency via cooperative means,*** fueled by the fires of the Open Source Movement.

Looking out across the invisible vistas of that rhizomatic parallel country we can begin to see our community beyond constraints, in the place where intention meets resilient, proactive, collaborative organization.

Here is a document born of that belief, sown purely of imagination and will. When we document we assert. We print to make real, to reify our being there. When we do so with mindful intention to address our process, to open our work to others, to create beauty in words in space, to respect and acknowledge the strength of the page we now hold physical, a thing in our hand, we remind ourselves that, like Dorothy: *we had the power all along, my dears.*

THE PRINT! DOCUMENT SERIES
is a project of
the trouble with bartleby
in collaboration with
the operating system

Lightning Source UK Ltd.
Milton Keynes UK
UKHW010642100521
383461UK00002B/313